# SEEKING
## THE
# CHRISTMAS LAMB

## A FAMILY ADVENT HANDBOOK

### FORTY DAYS OF CELEBRATING
### CHRIST'S SACRIFICE THROUGH THE SEASON

## TAMARA J. BUCHAN

HARDBACK ISBN: 978-0-692-54747-2
PAPERBACK ISBN: 978-0-692-55691-7

Some of the anecdotal illustrations in this book are true to life and are included with the permission of the persons involved. All other illustrations are composites of real situations, and any resemblance to people living or dead is coincidental.

Unless otherwise identified, all Scripture quotations in this publication are taken from the HOLY BIBLE: NEW INTERNATIONAL VERSION® (NIV®. Copyright © 1973, 1978, 1984 by International Bible Society. Used by permission of Zondervan Publishing House. All rights reserved. Other versions used include: the Holy Bible, New Living Translation, (NLT) copyright © 1996. Used by permission of Tyndale House Publishers, Inc., Wheaton, Illinois 60189. All rights reserved; and the New King James Version (NKJV). Copyright © 1982 by Thomas Nelson, Inc. Used by permission. All rights reserved.

Book illustration and cover design by Brenda Emmert and ebookannie.com.

## TO MY DEAR FAMILY:

Bill, your constant willingness to experiment and go along for the ride keeps our life a wonderful adventure. Heather, Bonnie, and Molly, celebrating Advent with you has been one of the greatest privileges of my life. It has brought me tremendous joy. I hope you will experience the same rich tradition with your own families one day.


## TO THE PEOPLE OF THE JOURNEY PROJECT:

Celebrating Advent together with you has been one of the highlights of my ministry. It was exciting to see how God opened all our eyes to see Him when we came together each week to celebrate! May you continue to enjoy the blessing of Advent God has for you.

*The Word became flesh and made his dwelling among us.*
*We have seen his glory, the glory of the One and Only,*
*who came from the Father, full of grace and truth.*

*John 1:14*

# CONTENTS

# PART ONE: ADVENT

## WEEK ONE: CREATION AND THE FALL

## WEEK TWO: THE SACRIFICIAL LAMB

## WEEK THREE: PROPHETS AND PROMISES

# WEEK FOUR: THE SAVIOR

# PART TWO: EPIPHANY

 # CELEBRATING THE TWELVE DAYS OF EPIPHANY

# PREFACE

Dear Friends,

This book comes to you with a full heart. As I have written it, I have been taken aback once again at the reality that the One who created the universe would invite me into relationship with Himself. I am loved by the Christmas Lamb; you are loved as well.

Writing the book came from a dream that was birthed in two places. The first was personal. Our family loves to celebrate Advent and was frustrated with the resources available. One day I finally tossed them aside and began to research in the Bible for myself why Jesus came to earth. The idea of the Christmas Lamb—or the Sacrificial Lamb, as Jesus also has been called—became clear. When we began to celebrate Advent with that idea in mind, I saw the light bulb go on in my kids' heads. They suddenly could connect all the different Bible stories they had been taught from their earliest days and understand why Jesus had to come to earth! Celebrating Advent and Epiphany has brought our family much closer together and has been a solid foundation from which our children have each made the decision to follow Jesus wherever He takes them.

Second, I was raised an evangelical, with no exposure to liturgy or the church year calendar. When I implemented a young children's worship program during my work as a children's pastor, I discovered the richness that comes from the church year. I realized that we miss something very special when we don't celebrate the high holy days. Lent--which starts with Ash Wednesday and culminates with Maundy Thursday, Good Friday, and Easter--is vital to our faith as Christians. Pentecost is the birth of the Christian church; it should be one of our greatest celebrations. The Advent and Epiphany season is a wonderful time to anticipate Christ's coming and the freedom He brings with His arrival.

I started a ministry called The Journey Project and together we discovered the richness of our faith as we combined the tenets of evangelicalism with the deep foundation of the church year and its liturgy. It was a blessing to watch the people of the Journey Project grow in the blessing that God wants for each one of us as we celebrate His gift of Jesus to us as the Sacrificial Lamb.

My hope is that this Advent and Epiphany season brings you closer to God's heart. May you be filled to overflowing joy as you prepare for His Son's birth and see Him as if for the first time. May you also wait expectantly for the day when He will come again—this time to take His children with Him. We look forward to that day.

God be with you,

Tamara J. Buchan

# INTRODUCTION

The Bible is a story. It begins in Genesis with the creation of the universe and continues with the creation of humanity—Adam and Eve, in particular. They lived in a perfect world until they made the grave mistake of eating the fruit from the Tree of Knowledge of Good and Evil. It was at this point that the perfect world God had created became filled with sin. Adam and Eve knew they had sinned, so they covered themselves with fig leaves. But God knew that they must be covered with blood and, therefore, made the first sacrifice of an animal that shed blood and then covered Adam and Eve with the skins from the animal.

This was a foreshadowing of the need for a permanent sacrifice, which eventually became Jesus. But until the proper time, the people of God were commanded to make animal sacrifices, which involved the "shedding of blood."

The book of Leviticus in the Old Testament is filled with rules for different sacrifices God required. They include the burnt offering, grain offering, fellowship offering, purification offering, and reparation offering

In this book, I'm calling Jesus "the Lamb," one of His many names. He is referred to as the "Lamb of God" several times throughout the story of the Bible. He is first called that name by John the Baptist in John 1:29: "Look, the Lamb of God, who takes away the sin of the world!" Old Testament prophets foretold his life and death and referred to Him as a lamb for sacrifice, as described by Isaiah in this well-known passage (Isaiah 53:7):

> *He was oppressed and afflicted,*
> *yet he did not open his mouth;*
> *he was led like a lamb to the slaughter,*
> *and as a sheep before her shearers is silent,*
> *so he did not open his mouth.*

A second mention of Jesus as the Lamb was made by Peter in the New Testament:

> *For you know that it was not with perishable things such as silver or gold*
> *that you were redeemed from the empty way of life handed down to you*

*from your forefathers, but with the precious blood of Christ, a lamb without
blemish or defect. He was chosen before the creation of the world, but was
revealed in these last times for your sake. (1 Peter 1:18-20)*

Jesus is also celebrated as the Lamb in Revelation. The apostle John described this vision: "Then I saw a Lamb, looking as if it had been slain, standing in the center of the throne" (Revelation 5:6).

The theme and symbol of the Sacrificial Lamb continues throughout the whole Bible—from the earliest days of humanity to the final throne in heaven. Jesus willingly came to earth at Christmas to become the Sacrificial Lamb. This Advent celebration will help clarify the story that has been given us. Praise be to God!

## A BRIEF HISTORY OF ADVENT AND EPIPHANY

What might a child's first reaction be if he were told that Christmas hasn't always taken place? Probably shock and disbelief. However, it's true. The celebration of Christmas started occurring long after the observance of Christ's death and resurrection. It wasn't until the fourth century that the church decided to observe Christ's birthday. Important leaders' birthdays during the Roman Empire traditionally were celebrated, so the Christians designated a feast day called "The Feast of the Nativity." It started with a special Mass to honor the remembrance of Jesus' coming they called "Christ's Mass." Eventually, it was shortened to "Christmas."

How did they decide on the date of December 25? No one knows the exact date Jesus was born. December 25 was introduced to Christians because it countered the pagan feast of the sun god, which was a popular winter festival held in Rome. The sun-god feast was held on December 21, the day when the sun shines the shortest time in the year, because the people wanted to coax the sun to come back! Christians found this time of the year to be the best to celebrate Christ's birth because although He was born into a dark world, He brought the world light. They wanted to draw people away from celebrating false gods to a place of celebrating the One True God.

Such a struggle between light and darkness has existed from the days of the Garden of Eden. When Adam and Eve stepped out of the perfect light and into darkness, they needed to be redeemed. God killed some of the animals He had created so Adam and Eve would have clothes to wear once they realized they were naked. The blood of the animals was the covering that God required, for where sin exists, so must blood for people to continue to be in relationship with God.

## ADVENT: PREPARING FOR HIS COMING

Waiting is a very important component of celebrating Advent. The people of Israel lived with the promise that God would return to them and the Messiah would set them free. How long the waiting seemed as they received promise after promise from Abraham, Moses, and the many prophets. More than four hundred years transpired with no word from God.

The season of Advent was designed to help us remember the "waiting." It comes from the Latin word for "coming." The season encompasses the four Sundays before Christmas, beginning around November 30. This structure echoes Old Testament festivals, which always included a specific number of days in preparation for a holy day.

In the tenth century, Advent was made the beginning of the liturgical year, which includes such celebrations as Epiphany, Lent, Easter, and Pentecost. This is fitting, as Advent is a time to start fresh, get ready, and prepare for the light to enter the darkness. It is a time for remembering that Jesus entered the dark world and brought hope and light and salvation.

Advent is not just a time to remember Christ's birth in Bethlehem; it is also a time to remember and prepare for Christ's Second Coming. He will return in all His glory to redeem those who believe, whether we are physically dead or alive, and take us back to heaven to live forever with Him.

## EPIPHANY: ALL PEOPLE MAY COME

The season of Epiphany runs from the day after Christmas, December 26, to the day of Epiphany, January 6. The feast day itself celebrates the manifestation of Christ to the Gentiles as represented by the wise men.

The Greek word from which epiphany is derived means "appearance, manifestation, showing forth." The wise men, who were invited by the star in the sky to seek the King, were the first Gentiles to ever worship the Lamb. Until that time, salvation was reserved for the covenant between God Almighty and His chosen people, the Jews.

Why is Epiphany important for us? We are also the Gentiles. We, like the wise men, were excluded from the covenant of salvation until the arrival of the Lamb. We were the foreigners who could not enter the temple to worship. We remained on the outside—until the Lamb came in all His glory and humility. Now we are invited into His presence, for worship, for salvation, for eternity.

The wise men didn't come empty-handed to see the baby Jesus. They came bearing gifts of gold, frankincense, and myrrh. The gold represented their wealth; it had economic value. The frankincense, from the resin of a desert tree, was a rare luxury. It was used by the high priests in worship. The myrrh had a sweet smell and a bitter taste, but it was a holy ointment used as a natural painkiller and to prepare a body for burial.

When we offer gifts to the Lamb, we are offering a sacrifice of our wealth, a sacrifice of worship to the Great High Priest, and a sacrifice of our bodies as living sacrifices to be used by the Lamb as He desires. It signifies we are willing to take up our cross daily and follow the Lamb.

Epiphany is a time for us to remember that we are included in God's plan of salvation. It is a time to look for all the ways the Lamb is explored, explained, celebrated, and worshiped throughout the New Testament. It is a time for God's people to rejoice.

The Christmas Lamb has arrived. His birth was revealed to shepherds on a hill caring for their flock, and it was revealed to Gentile kings from faraway lands. The celebration of Epiphany is ultimately a celebration acknowledging that the Lamb extends His grace and His blood beyond the chosen Jews. The Lamb also invites the Gentiles, those who are not of the Jewish race, to come and worship Him, approach His throne, and live with Him for eternity in heaven.

This book will take us from the point of Creation all the way to the celebration and worship of the Lamb at the throne. May God be with you as you prepare for the coming of the Lamb.

# HOW TO USE THIS BOOK

In the United States and many other countries, the holiday season (for most people, the period from Thanksgiving through New Year's Day) is jammed—with parties, shopping, school vacation, shopping, business events, family gatherings . . . and more shopping! If you've taken up this book, perhaps you feel the need to "tame" your holiday season and return it to its Source. How can you do that?

First, go look at your calendar. You're going to need to plan and prepare. Hopefully you've started early enough. If you're short on prep time, just do what you can. At least you'll be ahead, and there will always be next year.

Count back four Sundays from Christmas—this will be the first Sunday of Advent and is when you should start your readings. Epiphany season is a little easier, as it's always the twelve days from Christmas until January 6. Depending on the year, some of the Advent readings will overlap with the Epiphany readings.

Next, skim through the book to get a feel for what's coming. It's best to choose a regular time for your readings so your family starts expecting them. Do you all sit down together for supper? After you're through eating and before you start cleaning up might be a good time for your readings. Or perhaps you can manage to squeak out enough time at breakfast so as to send your family out into the day with their thoughts centered on their Savior. Think about what you'd like to accomplish with the Advent and Epiphany studies. If you're leading the celebrations with your family or a group of friends, ask them to describe their desires and goals as you journey together through Advent.

## GATHERING SUPPLIES

Collect the supplies you'll need. The children's activities may require a few simple items. At the start of each week, read through the "For Younger Children" sections to make sure you have everything you need to carry out the activity. And use your imagination! Do whatever it takes to make Advent celebrations memorable in your home—the aim is to grow closer to Jesus and love Him more by preparing for His coming birth.

**Here's a beginning list.**

**The Bible**. I like to use a version that sounds more like our daily conversations so it is more easily understood. Consider trying a new version you haven't used before as hearing a passage worded differently can bring new life to it. If you have small children it may be wise to use a children's Bible or to shorten or paraphrase the readings. In this technological age, I encourage you to use an actual "book" as there is something powerful about holding it in your hands, turning the pages to the Scripture and experiencing what generations of people have experienced through the ages.

**This book**. Use *Seeking the Christmas Lamb* each day to find the appropriate readings and to discuss the questions listed beneath each passage. Activities are included for families with younger children. We left room in each daily reading for you or your children to write significant thoughts or memories or for younger children to color a picture, making it a keepsake for your family!

**Advent wreath**. In ancient times a wreath was a symbol of victory and glory. The Christian Advent wreath symbolizes God's victory over sin and death, and the glory that Christ's birth shed light on humanity for all time. Traditionally, the wreath consists of candles in a circle of evergreen branches. Evergreen reminds us of the continuation of life and the promise of everlasting life in Jesus. The circle has no beginning or end, which suggests the eternal character and existence of God. The candles provide light and an inviting atmosphere in which to prepare for Christ's coming. They mark our waiting, as each week a new candle is lit. Three candles are purple, the liturgical color for Advent; one is pink, signifying purity. Alone in the center of the wreath is the Christ candle, representing the light Jesus brings. It should be white to remind us of His perfect sacrifice as the Lamb of God.

**Crèche or nativity scene**. This is especially important for use with young children. The crèche dates back to 1223. Francis of Assisi knew that because few people could read, the best way to tell the Christmas story was to act it out. He found a cave and picked out some animals and people to reenact the story. It was an instant hit! Soon, the idea spread all over Europe. Eventually, crèches as we know them today began to appear in people's homes to help them celebrate Jesus' birth. Leave the crèche empty until the last week when each day the children will add a person or character to the stable.

## HOLDING THE READINGS

First read the listed Scripture and the comments, and then finish with the reflection and discussion time. Pray and, if desired, sing a hymn or Christmas carol. Playing recorded music might bring added depth to your time together. Another fun option would be for any musically trained participants to pick up their instruments and accompany the group.

Before each Advent celebration, turn off the lights. This will remind everyone of how dark the world was before Jesus arrived on the scene, and it will also bring an added dimension to your time together. If possible, keep the lights off during the celebration and use a flashlight for the readings. Each week light one more candle so as it gets closer to Christmas, the light is much brighter than when you first began to celebrate Advent.

ADVENT

1

PART

# WEEK ONE

## CREATION AND THE FALL

FIRST SUNDAY IN ADVENT

FIRST MONDAY: Genesis 1:1-31

FIRST TUESDAY: Genesis 2:7-25

FIRST WEDNESDAY: Genesis 3:1-7

FIRST THURSDAY: Genesis 3:7-24

FIRST FRIDAY: Genesis 6:5–7:5

FIRST SATURDAY: Genesis 8:1; 8:13–9:17

## FIRST SUNDAY IN ADVENT

Light the first candle. Reread the introduction and the "How to Use This Book" section. Prepare any supplies you may need. Pray and celebrate that you are embarking on a wonderful journey as you prepare for Christmas!

# FIRST MONDAY:
# CREATION OF THE UNIVERSE

### *Genesis 1:1-31*

As you read this passage, did you hear words and phrases repeated? Did you notice how each day had its own purpose for Creation? Did you observe how God created just by "speaking His Word"? Did you catch what God said after each day of Creation? When God gets to the creation of humanity, after whom does He pattern it?

God gave people authority over all other living creatures––the fish of the sea and the birds of the air and every other living creature on the ground. He also gave every plant and tree with fruit to the   people as food. When all this was done, what did God say? Instead of His usual "it was good," verse 31 says, "God saw all that he had made, and it was very good."

The universe that God created was perfect. Can you picture God sitting back, admiring all He had made, and reveling in the glory of it all?

 REFLECT AND DISCUSS: Describe what you envision as the perfect life in the garden.

FOR YOUNGER CHILDREN:
Have clay available for making a world. As you shape the world, talk about the many different things God created, and then make some of them. Ask your children, "If you were Adam and Eve, what would have been your favorite part of the garden?"

NOTES:

# FIRST TUESDAY:
# THE COMPLETION
# AND THE COMMANDMENT

*Genesis 2:7-25*

The home God gave to Adam was one of terrific beauty and perfection. The Garden of Eden had four rivers that flowed out of the main river that watered the garden. In the very center of the paradise, God put two trees of great importance—the Tree of Life and the Tree of Knowledge of Good and Evil. God gave Adam and Eve complete freedom to partake of everything in the garden, except for one command: They were not to eat of the Tree of Knowledge of Good and Evil. The punishment for breaking God's command was severe: they would die.

Why did God do this? Why didn't He just give them freedom without any restraints? If He had, Adam and Eve would have been in a situation in which there was no need to choose God and obey Him. God wants us to choose Him.

Not only that. God desires to be in the center of every relationship, bringing people closer to each other and Himself. Humans, created in the image of the triune God, were made for relationships. Our deepest need is to be loved unconditionally. "It is not good for the man to be alone. I will make a helper suitable for him," God says in verse 18.

## REFLECT AND DISCUSS:

- How do you know you are created for relationship?
- What is the most important thing in your life?
- What brings you the greatest joy? What brings you the greatest sorrow?
- What makes the most significant memories for you?

 ## FOR YOUNGER CHILDREN:

Discuss the rules of your home, why you have those rules, and why it is important to follow them. List the rules on a poster or a plaque to post on your refrigerator. Talk about the one rule God gave to Adam and Eve.

NOTES:

 FIRST WEDNESDAY:
THE LIE

*Genesis 3:1-7*

What lies can you recognize from Satan, who disguised himself as the serpent? He made Eve doubt she had heard God's voice correctly. He also raised doubts about whether God had our best interests in mind when He gave the command to not eat from the tree.

Satan also deceived Eve into believing she could become like God if she ate from the tree. He led her to believe that God was holding out on her, that God wanted to control Adam and her. For just a moment, Eve forgot about the joyful relationship she had with God. She fell for the serpent's lies and ate the fruit. She also gave some fruit to Adam, who also did not resist the temptation; he ate too.

 REFLECT AND DISCUSS:

- What lies has the Enemy spoken to you?
- How have you responded to the lies?

FOR YOUNGER CHILDREN:

Ask them to recall a lie they may have heard their schoolmates tell. Have them remember how they responded.

- Did they believe the lie?
- Did they act on it?
- Or did they refuse to believe it and then walk away?

By reminding your kids about how Adam and Eve responded to the serpent, point out how easy it is to believe lies.

NOTES:

# FIRST THURSDAY: THE CONSEQUENCE

*Genesis 3:7-24*

Can you imagine the great sadness God must have had in His voice when He asked, "What is this you have done?" The perfect world God created was forever changed by Adam and Eve's decision to eat the fruit. They lost both their innocence and their freedom.

Living within God's boundaries provides us with freedom, not loss. The boundaries are there to protect us from harm. When Adam and Eve ignored the boundaries they were given, they lost everything. They lost perfect communion with God. They lost perfect relationship with each other. Suddenly, they knew they were naked and that they had to hide.

The reality is that from the very beginning of time, people have run to hide when they have either sinned or been sinned against. Until Adam and Eve ate the fruit, nothing stood between them and God. Their relationship with Him was free and simple. But their sin caused them to lose their innocence, and suddenly they were ashamed of their nakedness. They knew they needed to be covered up, so they put on the first thing that was familiar to them: bushes. However, bushes didn't make good coverings; they didn't fit in all the right places and Adam and Eve were very uncomfortable. They continued to hide.

How did God respond? Did He decide that since they disobeyed they were no longer worthy of His attention? No, God went looking for Adam and Eve. He called to them, asking, "Where are you?"

God always desires a relationship with us. He comes after us, but it is up to us how we will choose to respond. We can continue to hide in the bushes with the wrong coverings and ignore God's call. Or, we can answer Him and allow Him to give us the right coverings.

God made the first sacrifice that day. Verse 21 says God made garments of skin for Adam and Eve and clothed them. Do you realize that "garments of skin" means God killed an animal and blood was shed? From then on, animal sacrifices were to be the coverings for humanity until the true Lamb of God arrived.

REFLECT AND DISCUSS:

- What are God's boundaries in your life?
- Do you believe they protect you, or do you feel they get in the way of your freedom?
- How do you respond when you have either sinned or been sinned against?
- What false coverings do you wear? (For example: shame, materialism, isolation.)
- Imagine yourself in the garden. Would you have taken responsibility for your choice, or would you have made up an excuse?

 FOR YOUNGER CHILDREN:

Get out the plaque you made and discuss why each rule exists. Talk about the consequences of disobeying the rules. Look at how Adam and Eve responded to their choice to disobey God's rule. Decide if they responded appropriately or if they blamed others. Point out how God responded to their choice. How does God respond to our choices?

NOTES:

# FIRST FRIDAY:
# THE FLOOD

*Genesis 6:5–7:5*

Have you ever done something, and then after a while, you just wanted to start over? This must be where God was in the sixth chapter of Genesis. He had created a perfect world, but after sin entered it, it was filled with evil, pain, and destruction.

Genesis 6:6 says, "The Lord was grieved that he had made [humanity] on the earth, and his heart was filled with pain." Genesis 6:13 tells us what God chose to do with His grief and pain. "God said to Noah, 'I am going to put an end to all   people, for the earth is filled with violence because of them. I am surely going to destroy both them and the earth.'"

Many of us have been taught that God was so angered He wanted to destroy what He had created. Another conclusion is this: God was so in favor of what He had created that He was providing a second chance. He was providing a way of escape for a world that had become too wicked for its own existence. He raised up Noah, a mere human, to accomplish His purposes. Basically, Noah was given the opportunity to save a remnant, but it came at a great cost. It took a long time to build such a huge ark and it never had rained before. So how did Noah explain his activity to others? He may have never been able to explain what he was doing, but that did not deter him from following what God asked him to do. He just kept building.

 REFLECT AND DISCUSS:

- What has God asked you to do that didn't seem to make sense?
- How did you respond?
- If you followed through with it, what was the outcome?
- If you didn't follow through, think about what you might have missed out on.

Pray for the courage to follow through with your next assignment.

FOR YOUNGER CHILDREN:

Find an empty box with which to create an ark. Talk about how long it took Noah to make the ark and how he had to do it by the exact instructions that God gave to him. Talk about how important it is for your children to live by your instructions and the instructions that the Bible gives. Then, give your kids step-by-step directions for making the ark. If they get a bit frustrated, use the moment to help them realize how difficult it was for Noah to follow God's commands.

NOTES:

# FIRST SATURDAY: GOD REMEMBERS

## *Genesis 8:1; 8:13–9:17*

The earth had now been rinsed clean by the Flood. Noah and his family were in the ark, waiting for 150 long days for the water to recede. However, we see something new and fresh in Genesis 8:1, where it says, "But God remembered Noah and all the wild animals and the livestock that were with him in the ark, and he sent a wind over the earth, and the waters receded."

God knew two truths at this point. He knew that humankind was hopeless. Creation had not changed. It was deeply set against God's purposes. Hope would not come from a change of behavior; it would have to come from a move of God. Second, God cast a new royal decree. God let humanity know that He would stay with, endure, and sustain His world, despite what humanity chose to do.[1]

It was at the point that Noah disembarked from the ark that blood once again entered the picture. Noah built an altar to the Lord and sacrificed some of the animals he kept so carefully through the Flood. It was when God observed Noah's sacrificial act of offering animals he had so carefully preserved on the ark that God declared He would never again curse the ground or destroy all creation.

God also reinforced the high value of human life when He demanded an accounting for any murder that occurred. He reminded Noah that people are created in God's image, and that each life is of ultimate value. Anyone who took a life would give a life in payment.

The final promise, the rainbow, was a physical sign that God remembers. The only thing the waters of chaos and death did not cut through was a commitment of God to creation. His remembering was an act of gracious engagement with His covenant partner, an act of committed compassion. It asserted that God was not preoccupied with Himself but with His covenant partner, creation. It is the remembering of God, and only that, which gives hope and makes new life possible. The God who rules over us has turned toward us in a new way.[2]

REFLECT AND DISCUSS: Recall the elements in this passage—waiting, God remembering, His "change of mind" (from our viewpoint), and His covenant promise of the rainbow. Apply them to your own life.

- Have you ever waited for something for a very long time?
- Did you feel as if God had deserted you? How did you respond?
- Was there a point in which you felt that God did remember?
- Did you "build an altar" to help you remember that God was present all along?

This gesture could mean writing an account of God's actions, telling another person, artistically creating something about it, or praying a special prayer.

FOR YOUNGER CHILDREN: Color a rainbow and put it up as a reminder that God keeps His promises.

NOTES:

# WEEK TWO

# 2

## THE SACRIFICIAL LAMB

SECOND SUNDAY IN ADVENT

SECOND MONDAY: Genesis 22:1-18

SECOND TUESDAY: Exodus 12:1-14

SECOND WEDNESDAY: Exodus 12:21-41

SECOND THURSDAY: Exodus 20:1-24

SECOND FRIDAY: Leviticus 4:32-35; 5:5-7; 17:1-11
or Numbers 28:1-16

SECOND SATURDAY: 1 Kings 8:1-11

# SECOND SUNDAY IN ADVENT

Light the second candle today. Catch up on any readings that you may have missed last week. Come to a place of worship and celebrate with those who also are observing Advent.

# SECOND MONDAY: THE PROVISION

### *Genesis 22:1-18*

How do you feel right before you take a test? Is your stomach queasy? Are your palms sweaty? Are you confident about your preparation, or do you wish for just a few more hours to study?

This passage starts out with a test. Abraham didn't have any time to get ready for it, though. He had to respond quickly. The problem was that his test involved God's promise to him. God had promised him that he would have so many descendants that they would be more numerous than sand on the seashore. He also waited twenty-five years just to have one child, let alone a sandbox full! Now God was asking him to give the child, Isaac, back.

Abraham must have been ready for his test, however. The very next morning he left with Isaac to go to the mountain. Would you have been able to respond that quickly?

When Abraham and Isaac left the servants behind and began to walk up the mountain with the firewood, the flint, and the knife,   Abraham's heart must have been heavy. He must have been wondering, What are you doing, God? but he kept walking, putting one step in front of another. Suddenly, Isaac asked, "Where is the lamb for the sacrifice?" Amazingly, prophetically, Abraham said, "God will provide the lamb."

 Can you hear the words echoing across the centuries? God will provide the lamb!

"When the time had fully come, God sent his Son, born of a woman, born under law, to redeem those under law, that we might receive the full rights of sons" (Galatians 4:4-5). God sent Jesus to be our sacrifice, the Lamb of God who takes away the sins of the world.

Just as Isaac was about to die, God intervened. He sent a sacrifice, a ram stuck in the bushes. Isaac didn't have to die, and neither do we.

**REFLECT AND DISCUSS:**

- What does it mean to have the Lamb of God as the perfect sacrifice?
- How does it change your life?

 **FOR YOUNGER CHILDREN:**

Draw a large lamb on a piece of paper. Have your children paste cotton balls on the picture for the wool. Talk about how God provided a sacrifice so Abraham didn't have to sacrifice his son Isaac. Ask your children if God has ever provided them with something they needed. (Be ready with suggestions if they can't think of anything.)

**NOTES:**

 SECOND TUESDAY:
THE PASSOVER

### Exodus 12:1-14

Imagine the scene. All of the Israelites outside of their houses at the same time, slaughtering the lamb that has lived in their home for the past two weeks. Imagine the blood running down the streets. Imagine the blood being painted over the doorways. Imagine the faith it took to carry out all of God's commands. Imagine standing while you eat with your cloak tucked into your belt, sandals on and staff in hand. Imagine what it felt like to go to bed that night, knowing that the next sacrifice would be the oldest male of each Egyptian household.

What was the purpose of the blood over the doorframes? Protection. Houses with blood posted on the doorframes were protected when the angel of death "passed over" them.

Jesus' blood protects us from death as well. When we decide to follow Him, we are cleansed with His blood. This is the cleansing that gives us eternal life; we are protected from eternal death.

> But God showed his great love for us by sending Christ to die for us while we were still sinners. And since we have been made right in God's sight by the blood of Christ, he will certainly save us from God's judgment. For since we were restored to friendship with God by the death of his Son while we were still his enemies, we will certainly be delivered from eternal punishment by his life. (Romans 5:8-10, NLT)

**REFLECT AND DISCUSS:**

Think about what it would have been like to be one of the Israelites. You would have seen all the miracles that had occurred, and yet you would still have been a slave. Then the time would have come when God said, "Get ready!"

- Would you be excited? Would you be cynical? Would you be afraid? Would you be sad to leave Egypt? Would you believe?
- What is it that God is calling you to get ready for today?
- How are you responding?

 **FOR YOUNGER CHILDREN:**

Talk about the last trip that you took. What did you do to get ready? What did you take? Talk about how the Israelites got ready and what they left behind. Talk about how much they had to trust God to be able to get ready. Tomorrow night, eat dinner with your coats on and standing up. Practice being ready to go where God asks you to go.

**NOTES:**

 SECOND WEDNESDAY:
THE EXODUS

### Exodus 12:21-41

Think about what this passage is describing. More than a million people leaving Egypt, no longer slaves, but free people! Imagine the waves and waves of people leaving the place where they and their ancestors had lived for 430 years. Envision Egyptians, who had been their enslavers, throwing money and clothing at them, begging them just to leave. Picture house after empty house, street after street, with only the blood on the doorways to set them apart.

What does the blood bring in *this* passage?

In the previous passage, the blood brought protection, but in this reading, the blood brought freedom. Not only were the occupants of the houses that displayed the blood not touched, they also were released from their slavery.

 **REFLECT AND DISCUSS:**

Take a moment to dwell on how Jesus' blood gives you freedom.

 **FOR YOUNGER CHILDREN:**

Weather permitting, go outside and pretend you are one of a million people leaving home. What would it feel like to leave your room behind? What would it be like to leave your toys, and your pets, and your bike? How do you think the Israelite children felt leaving their homes behind?

**NOTES:**

 # SECOND THURSDAY: THE TEN COMMANDMENTS

## *Exodus 20:1-24*

Have you ever visited a foreign country or spent time with someone from another culture? Perhaps you've been confronted with a plethora of unfamiliar practices and customs and felt uncertain or uncomfortable. There's always the possibility of making a big cultural error when you're not sure how things are done.

The Israelites were in a new place. They were no longer slaves; they were nomads, traveling in the desert. In Egypt, they knew the rules. They knew who was in charge and whom to obey. But once they were free, they were no longer sure of what the rules were, or whom to follow.

God didn't let them wonder long. He came to the Israelites and told them the rules, rules designed to protect and guide them and keep them close to God's heart. We now know those rules as the Ten Commandments.

After God had given these Rules for Right Living and the people had backed away in fear of God, He added one more reminder. It's much like parents calling out when their children leave the house: "Don't forget your coat. Remember to take your driver's license. Be careful." God ordered them to not make other gods, for He is the One True God. Then He commanded them to make an altar and sacrifice burnt offerings and fellowship offerings to signify the importance of receiving the Ten Commandments.

 **REFLECT AND DISCUSS:**
- What would you do if you had moved to a new culture or country?
- Would you learn the language first?
- Would you seek out the market or get a driver's license or find the schools?
- Would you adapt to the customs and incorporate the celebrations of the culture?

Now put yourself in the Israelites' place as they were adapting to their new surroundings.
- Do you think the Ten Commandments, or the Rules for Right Living, gave them security because they had new boundaries in which to live?

**FOR YOUNGER CHILDREN:**

Go through the Ten Commandments and put them into simple words. Help your children understand God gave these rules to help them to learn to honor Him as well as treat their friends, family, and neighbors kindly. Have them pick one rule to work on in the next week.

**NOTES:**

 SECOND FRIDAY:
SACRIFICES

## Leviticus 4:32-35; 5:5-7; 17:1-11 or Numbers 28:1-16

It is apparent from the instructions given in these passages that sacrifice was to be taken seriously. It was to be done with the proper animals, techniques, and people at the proper place. In fact, if the requirements of where a sacrifice was made were not followed, that person was cut off from the rest of the Israelites (see Leviticus 17:8-9). How severe! It was much like our laws today. If someone breaks the law, he is sent to prison to be set apart from the rest of the culture.

The book of Leviticus starts off by explaining the different offerings: the burnt offering, grain offering, fellowship offering, sin offering, and guilt offering. These offerings were to be taken seriously. After they are introduced in the first five chapters of Leviticus, they are brought up again in chapters six and seven with further instructions. We often wonder why God had such stringent requirements for the sacrifices. Eugene Peterson introduces Leviticus this way in his Bible version *The Message: The Old Testament Books of Moses:*

> *The book of Leviticus is a narrative pause in the story of our ancestors as they are on their way, saved out of Egypt, to settle in the land of Canaan. It is a kind of extended time-out of instruction, a detailed and meticulous preparation for living "holy" in a culture that doesn't have the faintest idea what holy is. The moment these people enter Canaan they will be picking their way through a lethal mine field of gods and goddesses that are designed to appeal to our god-fantasies. "Give us what we want when we want it on our own terms." What these god-fantasies in fact do is cripple or kill us. Leviticus is a start at the "much teaching and long training" that continues to be adapted and reworked in every country and culture where God is forming a saved people to live as he created them to live—holy as God is holy!*
>
> *The first thing that strikes us as we read Leviticus in this light is that this holy God is actually present with us and virtually every detail of our lives is affected by the presence of this holy God; nothing in us, our relationships, or environment is left out. The second thing is that God provides a way (the sacrifices and feast and Sabbaths) to bring everything in and about us into his holy presence, transformed in the fiery blaze of the holy. It is an awesome thing to come into his presence and we, like ancient Israel, stand in his presence at every moment.[3]*

We understand from Genesis 3 that God requires blood to cover sin. He killed the animals to cover Adam and Eve—they wore the fur, but it was the blood that allowed them to stay in relationship with the God Almighty. Over and over again in the first books of the Old Testament, we are reminded of the importance of shed blood to cover sin. We are told in these passages that the blood must be shed correctly and that if it is eaten, the penalty is separation from people and from God. This seems strange to us in our culture in which some of us love a rare steak that is seeping in blood. Why is the shedding of blood to cover sin mentioned in the Bible so many times? It is because God was setting the stage for the perfect sacrifice.

Jesus is the final sacrificial lamb, and we need to understand that His sacrifice was done according to God's just ways to satisfy God's just nature. Jesus' blood is so precious that we are covered in the robes of righteousness, always to be looked upon by a just God as forgiven and perfectly clean, as stated by John in 1 John 1:7 and 2:1-2:

> *But if we walk in the light, as [Jesus] is in the light, we have fellowship with one another, and the blood of Jesus, his Son, purifies us from all sin. . . . [Also] My dear children, I write this to you so that you will not sin. But if anybody does sin, we have one who speaks to the Father in our defense—Jesus Christ, the Righteous One. He is the atoning sacrifice for our sins, and not only for ours but also for the sins of the whole world.*

**REFLECT AND DISCUSS:**

Take a moment to dwell on how Jesus' blood gives you freedom.

**FOR YOUNGER CHILDREN:**

Read the verses in 1 John listed above and explain to your children how Jesus is the one that makes us right with God. Explain that His blood shed from the cross made Him the perfect sacrifice. Ask them if they would like to confess a sin, and then thank Jesus for making forgiveness from God possible.

**NOTES:**

# SECOND SATURDAY: A GRAND BUILDING DEDICATION

## *1 Kings 8:1-11*

Can you imagine the excitement? It was moving day for all Israelites' spiritual life. They had waited their entire history for a permanent place to worship. They had waited thirteen years for the construction of the temple, and finally it was finished. It is significant that the timing of the move was during the Feast of Tabernacles. This feast celebrated God granting rest to His people in the Promised Land and also was a renewal time for the covenant of the Ten Commandments. The Israelites would move from worshiping in a mobile tabernacle to a permanent place at the temple.

Have you ever been to a dedication of an important building? The dedication doesn't take place until all the dignitaries have arrived. It is the same in this passage. After all the men of Israel and the priests had gathered--including, of course, King Solomon-- the dedication began. The pinnacle of the dedication involved bringing the ark of the covenant from Zion, the City of David, to its permanent home in the temple in Jerusalem. The ark held manna from the wilderness and the Ten Commandments Moses had received from God.

This passage is a culmination of a large segment of time for the Israelites. Adam and Eve were covered with furs from the first sacrificed animals; Moses received the Ten Commandments on stone written by fire from God after the Israelites had supernaturally been set free from the Egyptians; and the Israelites continued to wait 480 years to have their own permanent place to worship, having the ark of the covenant as their only lasting symbol to revere.

Part of the celebration for dedicating the temple involved sacrificing so many animals that they couldn't be counted. The final item to be brought into the temple was the ark of the covenant. When all of the above had been done and the priests had left the Holy Place, a cloud filled the temple: the cloud of God's glory. It was so powerful that the priests had to stop performing their service; they had to just worship. This was a foreshadowing of what happens in the New Testament. When Jesus came as the perfect sacrifice, He told us to stop working and to rest and worship in His presence.

*"Come to me, all you who are weary and burdened, and I will give you rest. Take my yoke upon you and learn from me, for I am gentle and humble in heart, and you will find rest for your souls. For my yoke is easy and my burden is light." (Matthew 11:28-30)*

### REFLECT AND DISCUSS:

Think about what it would have been like to be one of the priests serving in the temple.

- How would it have changed your life to be in a place of worship that was so filled with the glory of the Lord that you were moved to your knees in total awe and reverence?
- Is there an area in your life in which Jesus is calling you to stop working and to rest?

### FOR YOUNGER CHILDREN:

Draw a picture of the temple. Have them include the ark of the covenant and the priests being moved to worship. Hang the pictures in a prominent place to remind you that God invites us to rest and worship Him.

### NOTES:

# WEEK THREE

## PROPHETS AND PROMISES

THIRD SUNDAY IN ADVENT

THIRD MONDAY: Isaiah 53:1-12

THIRD TUESDAY: Jeremiah 31:27-34

THIRD WEDNESDAY: Isaiah 56:1-8

THIRD THURSDAY: Isaiah 43:16-26

THIRD FRIDAY: 2 Samuel 12:1-13

THIRD SATURDAY: Psalm 51:1-17

# THIRD SUNDAY IN ADVENT

Light the third candle today. Catch up on any readings you may have missed last week. Come to a place of worship to celebrate with others who are also observing Advent.

Say a prayer of thanks to Jesus Christ, who is the Lamb sacrificed not only for you but also for the whole world, as explained in John 3:16: "For God so loved the world that He gave His only begotten Son, that whoever believes in Him should not perish but have everlasting life" (NKJV).

# THIRD MONDAY:
# THE SUFFERING SERVANT

## *Isaiah 53:1-12*

Have you ever looked and looked for something that you lost, but couldn't find it? And then you eventually find out it was right in front of you the whole time? That must be what it was like for the Jews in Jesus' day. They were so sure of what they were looking for in the Messiah that when He didn't match their expectations, they couldn't see Him to save their lives!

The Israelites were looking for a triumphant ruler who would bring them to religious and political freedom. They envisioned a mighty king who would arrive on white horseback with hundreds following behind him and destroy the Romans who had been enslaving the Israelites. They couldn't imagine one who wouldn't seek to destroy their enslavers on earth, and do it with a great display of power.

This passage in Isaiah points to a different way: it is the way of a suffering servant.

Almost every verse in this chapter speaks of another way the Messiah will suffer. Perhaps that is why the passage begins with "Who has believed our message . . . " Who would believe that the God of the Universe would allow—no, ordain—His Son to set aside His godly status and become a servant who willingly suffers. For whom? Could it be for humanity? Could it be for the Israelites? Could it be for the Gentiles as well? Could it even be for you and for me?

### REFLECT AND DISCUSS:

Take a moment to write down all the words that involve suffering. Read them aloud, pondering what each word involves. Consider that Jesus is the one who willingly gave Himself as the perfect sacrifice. Write or say a prayer of thanks for what it cost Him.

### FOR YOUNGER CHILDREN:

Remember with your children some of their "owies" or injuries. Talk about how much they hurt. Then talk about how much Jesus physically suffered by being the perfect sacrifice for us.

**NOTES:**

 THIRD TUESDAY:
THE NEW COVENANT

## Jeremiah 31:27-34

Last week we studied the passage in 1 Kings that describes the dedication and consecration of the temple. Now in the story, a few hundred years had passed, the temple had been destroyed, and the Jews were watching another destruction occur—this time, the destruction of all of Jerusalem. Most of the Jerusalem people were being transported to Babylon to become slaves.

The news coming from the prophet Jeremiah was, for the most part, not good news. However, in chapter 31 Jeremiah did have some good news. The Lord declared that just as He watched over the uprooting and the tearing down, the overthrowing, the destruction, and the disaster, so He would also watch over them to build and to plant. Building and planting were extremely important to the Jews, as buildings brought roofs over their heads, and planting brought them food to eat. But that wasn't even the best news; more good news followed.

God was establishing a New Covenant. The Israelites were enduring suffering due to their failure to live up to the covenant that God established with Moses—the Ten Commandments. The laws were external and the Israelites had failed to follow them. But now God was bringing a new way: the law would be planted internally—it would be put in their minds and written on their hearts. Everyone, not just the house of Israel and the house of Judah, would know the Lord. It would no longer be a hierarchy, because all, from the least to the greatest, would know the Lord.

Jesus fulfilled this prophecy by offering His blood in the perfect sacrifice, as demonstrated in 1 Corinthians 11:23-26, a passage on Communion. Jesus states in verse 25: "This cup is the new covenant in my blood; do this, whenever you drink it, in remembrance of me." The blood Jesus shed offers a lost world a new way. It offers the chance to know the Lord by having Christ's law of love put in our minds and written on our hearts.

**REFLECT AND DISCUSS:**

Take a moment to write down all the words that involve suffering. Read them aloud, pondering what each word involves. Consider that Jesus is the one who willingly gave Himself as the perfect sacrifice. Write or say a prayer of thanks for what it cost Him.

 **FOR YOUNGER CHILDREN:**

Remember with your children some of their "owies" or injuries. Talk about how much they hurt. Then talk about how much Jesus physically suffered by being the perfect sacrifice for us.

**NOTES:**

# THIRD WEDNESDAY:
# THE BOUNDARIES EXPAND

## *Isaiah 56:1-8*

We studied earlier how strict the rules for worship and sacrifice were for the Israelites in the beginning. Deuteronomy 23:1 states this: "No one who has been emasculated by crushing or cutting may enter the assembly of the Lord." The Israelites did not condone the making of eunuchs, but it was a common practice in other cultures. So those taken captive and made to be eunuchs also suffered exclusion from worship in the temple. They were considered "unclean" because they had been cut as a sign they were set apart to serve other rulers. Thus they could not enter the place of God's holiness.

Realizing how drastic the measures were to maintain purity can bring us a much greater appreciation of what the New Covenant means to us today. Not only did Christ's sacrifice open the door for eunuchs and anyone considered "unclean" to worship him freely (see Acts 8:26-39), but it opened the door for us too. We are the foreigners to whom this passage refers. We are the ones who, if we bind ourselves to the Lord—to serve Him, to love His name, and to worship Him—and who, if we keep the Sabbath without desecrating it, will be invited to God's holy mountain and given joy in our places of worship!

What does this mean to you? How can God accept us when He established such stringent rules? Because Jesus provided the perfect sacrifice. His blood makes it possible for us to stand before God and be looked on as sinless. His blood makes it possible for us to worship freely without restraint. His blood makes it possible to approach God in prayer—in our churches, living rooms, cars, laundry rooms, and workplaces. His blood sets us free!

### REFLECT AND DISCUSS:

Think about what it means to have the boundaries of God's chosen people expanded from just clean Israelites to all people, everywhere! How can you be a part of expanding the boundaries of Jesus to others?

**FOR YOUNGER CHILDREN:**

Take the wrapped gift to the person you and your children picked out during the last reading. When you go, have your children express they came because they wanted to share the love of Jesus.

**NOTES:**

 THIRD THURSDAY:
THE NEW WAY

### *Isaiah 43:16-26*

God did many miraculous things in the Israelites' history. He released the captives from Egypt, and when they were pressed up against the Red Sea with no perceived way of escape, He provided a way to freedom. He drew back the water for the Israelites to pass through, and when they were safely across the sea and the Egyptian army was entering, the waters came crashing down and the enemy was drowned. God provided a way where there seemed to be no way.

Now He was telling the Israelites to forget that miracle—He was going to do something much bigger than protecting them from an army. He realized their need for a miracle went much deeper than physical safety. They needed to be forgiven for their sinful attitudes and actions. The Israelites had forsaken their sacrifices of animals and grain offerings and incense. They hadn't given God their best. When life got easier, they forgot God and His miracles.

But, amazingly, we serve a God who never gives up. He provides the miracle of Living Water—we will be refreshed, we will be forgiven, we will be vibrant forever as we live with Christ.

### REFLECT AND DISCUSS:

Perhaps God is calling you to forget the past and see Him doing a new thing in your life. Is it possible there is an area in your life for which God has forgiven you, but you cannot forget or forgive yourself? Hebrews 9:14 says this:

> *How much more, then, will the blood of Christ, who through the eternal Spirit offered himself unblemished to God, cleanse our consciences from acts that lead to death, so that we may serve the living God!*

**FOR YOUNGER CHILDREN:**

Talk about how God forgives our sins and doesn't remember them anymore. Turn to Psalm 103:11-13 and read how God literally removes our sins from us. After reading the verses, have your children write down something they have been feeling guilty about (don't look, this is between them and God). Have them put it in a paper bag and take it out to the trash, never to be seen or thought of again!

**NOTES:**

 # THIRD FRIDAY: THE PET LAMB

## 2 Samuel 12:1-13

King David was known as "a man after God's own heart." But that is hard to believe when you read of this scene between the prophet Nathan and David. Nathan accused him of murder and adultery. Does that sound like a man who resembles God's character?

The story is a powerful allegory. A poor man had raised a pet lamb from infancy. He was very attached to the lamb. The rich man had herds of cattle and a load of sheep, kept by hired shepherds. They held no value to the rich man, except the price for which he could sell them.

When a houseguest came to visit, the rich man stole the poor man's precious pet lamb and proudly served it to the houseguest, all the while thinking about how shrewd he was to not have had to sacrifice one of his animals.

David did that very act. Out of hundreds of women to choose from he sought a married woman—Bathsheba. While her husband was away at war, David got Bathsheba pregnant. David was caught. Instead of acting with integrity, he had the husband killed at the front. He then married Bathsheba. As the child was born around the time Nathan came to David, we know David had lived with this sin for many months, probably over a year.

What is the point of this story? Perhaps it is to show us that we all sin--even those of us who have a heart after God. It is part of who we are; no one is immune. It is how we respond that matters.

David could have had the prophet Nathan killed for stating something he didn't want to hear. However, David instantly replied, "I have sinned against the Lord." He recognized his sin and he repented. This is what made David "a man after God's own heart."

**REFLECT AND DISCUSS:**

- How do you respond when you are confronted?
- Do you listen and say you are sorry, or do you get defensive?
- When you sin, do you distance yourself from God, or do you run to Him for forgiveness?

Ask God to give you a "heart like His own."

 **FOR YOUNGER CHILDREN:**

Have your children each hold a favorite stuffed animal while you talk about the story. Suddenly, take each animal away. Ask your children how they felt after losing the animal. Talk about how important it is for them to share their many blessings and possessions willingly with others. Pray with them and ask God to give them generous hearts.

**NOTES:**

# THIRD SATURDAY:
# A BROKEN SPIRIT

### Psalm 51:1-17

This is the psalm that King David wrote after his confrontation with the prophet Nathan. David boldly asked for God's mercy and forgiveness. He even went into detail about how he would like to be cleansed—with the hyssop, a strongly scented flowering plant of the mint family. The twigs were used for sprinkling liquid. Hyssop was used to sprinkle blood over the doorframes at the first Passover. David was asking God to sprinkle blood over him, as he knew that ultimately it is blood that brings forgiveness.

However, it is interesting to note that David ended this writing by saying:

> *O Lord, open my lips,*
> *and my mouth will declare your praise.*
> *You do not delight in sacrifice, or I would bring it;*
> *you do not take pleasure in burnt offerings.*
> *The sacrifices of God are a broken spirit;*
> *a broken and contrite heart,*
> *O God, you will not despise. (15-17)*

David understood that what God ultimately wants from us is relationship. He wants our hearts. He wants us to run to Him when we have made mistakes or sinned deeply. He wants to put His arms around us, hold us tight, and assure us that we are okay, because Jesus is the Perfect Sacrificial Lamb, and with His blood, we are clean and forgiven in His eyes.

**REFLECT AND DISCUSS:**

Reread today's passage, with the aim of making it personal. When you read "I," let it be your "I." Then close your eyes and envision God fully embracing you as you give Him your sacrifices of a broken and contrite heart.

**FOR YOUNGER CHILDREN:**

Have your children either write or dictate a letter regarding how it felt to put their sins in the paper bag to throw them away permanently. If they would like to send it to someone special in their lives, do so; otherwise, save the letter for a day when they are being hard on themselves and pull it out to remind them of what God's forgiveness feels like—clean, permanent, and free!

**NOTES:**

# WEEK FOUR

## THE SAVIOR

FOURTH SUNDAY IN ADVENT

FOURTH MONDAY: Luke 1:26-56

FOURTH TUESDAY: Matthew 1:18-25

FOURTH WEDNESDAY: Luke 2:1-20

FOURTH THURSDAY: Luke 2:21-39

FOURTH FRIDAY: Matthew 2:1-23

FOURTH SATURDAY: John 1:1-37

FOURTH SUNDAY IN ADVENT

Light the fourth candle today. Count off the number of days until Christmas, and do one of two things: Double up some days, or work backward, reading only the days that will cause you to finish with Christmas Day.

Catch up on any readings you missed last week, or read ahead! Then, come and celebrate with others who love the Savior as well.

# FOURTH MONDAY: MARY

*Luke 1:26-56*

Mary was a very young woman when she was confronted by the angel Gabriel. She may have only been fourteen or fifteen years old, but she was faced with the biggest decision of her life that day. She had to decide whether she would carry the Messiah within her body. Her decision would impact eternity.

Mary didn't have all the answers. She didn't understand how she could become pregnant when she was a virgin. She innocently asked the angel Gabriel how such a thing could be a reality. The angel Gabriel responded finally by saying, "Nothing is impossible with God."

Indeed, nothing is impossible with God. Nor is He predictable. His miracles usually occur in times and ways we least expect—oftentimes when they are least convenient. Sometimes they come to those we would least expect. Mary didn't have control over what God chose to do; she had control only over her response. She responded by acknowledging that God was her leader and that she would willingly go along with His plan.

After the awe and amazement wore off, Mary must have become afraid. How would she tell Joseph? How would she tell her parents? Who would believe the wild story? But in the midst of her fear, God provided a place of safety.

The angel Gabriel mentioned Mary's older cousin Elizabeth because she was also involved in the miracle of new birth. Elizabeth was carrying the prophet John the Baptist—the one who was appointed to prepare God's people for Jesus' arrival on earth.

Mary decided to go to Elizabeth. When she entered Elizabeth's house, she was given confirmation that she was not dreaming, that she was not crazy, and that she truly was carrying the Messiah. Elizabeth yelled out, "Blessed are you among women, and blessed is the child you will bear!"

Imagine the three months that Mary and Elizabeth spent together. They most likely dreamed together for the futures of their miraculous children. Perhaps they asked each other what God would do next. Surely they were able to comfort and encourage one another.

When the time came for Mary to go home, she returned not as a scared young girl but as a woman--ready to face her future, ready to bear the Messiah, ready to offer hope

REFLECT AND DISCUSS:

- How would you have responded if you were Mary?
- What do you think Mary and Elizabeth dreamed about and talked about together?
- What would it have been like to be Mary returning to her home?
- What would you have thought about on the trip back to Galilee?

FOR YOUNGER CHILDREN:

Take your empty stable and add the animals and Mary. Reenact the scene with the angel and how Mary responded. Keep the crèche close by to add people to each day.

NOTES:

# FOURTH TUESDAY: JOSEPH

*Matthew 1:18-25*

Then Mary came back to Galilee and began the painful task of telling the important people in her life she was pregnant. Imagine the scene between Mary and her fiancé, Joseph. See her describing the visitation and her resulting pregnancy. Joseph, who loved Mary and did not want to hurt her, must have been very conflicted. Agonize with him as he decides to break the engagement quietly, because a public renouncement would lead to humiliation and perhaps even death by stoning.

While he considered all this, probably wondering how his very reasonable Mary could have ever come up with such a wild tale, he also was confronted by an angel! The angel assured him that Mary wasn't crazy or a wild tale-teller--she was about to have a child, and the child was the Messiah. The angel told him, "Go and marry her. Do not be afraid. Do not hesitate!"

Joseph immediately did what the angel told him to do. As soon as he woke up, he went and took Mary to be his wife. He did not hesitate. He did not count the cost, but there likely was one. It may have cost him customers. It may have cost him the support and love of his family. It may have cost him his home, as the people in his town ostracized both Mary and Joseph because she was pregnant before she married him.

**REFLECT AND DISCUSS:**

- Has God ever asked you to do something that had a big cost attached to it?
- How did you respond?

 **FOR YOUNGER CHILDREN:**

Put Joseph in the stable along with Mary and the animals. Talk about what it must have been like for them to wait for the baby Jesus to be born.

NOTES:

# FOURTH WEDNESDAY: THE SHEPHERDS

*Luke 2:1-20*

Everything in the Bible is there for a reason. Why did Mary, nine months pregnant, have to ride a donkey for three or four days and deliver her baby in Bethlehem? Why was Jesus born in a stable, alongside animals, instead of in an inn, where it would be more comfortable? Why did the angels choose shepherds to whom to make their announcement that the Savior had been born?

These were not random events. Bethlehem was significant because of the prophecy in Micah 5:2 that "one who will be ruler over Israel will come from Bethlehem." Bethlehem was also the town in which shepherds raised sheep destined for sacrifice at the temple. How appropriate that Jesus was born in the town known for sacrificial lambs, as His ultimate calling was to be the "perfect, eternal sacrificial lamb."

Joseph and Mary's reputation had preceded them, and no one would dare to ruin his good name by housing such people of low character and morals. Jesus states in Matthew 8:20 that "foxes have holes and birds of the air have nests, but the Son of Man has no place to lay his head." Whatever the human circumstances, Jesus was born in a stable because He was sent to suffer for the world. His birth in a stable was a foreshadowing of the life He would lead on earth and the life to which He calls His followers.

Finally, the angels revealed their glory and announced the good news to shepherds. Shepherds held the lowest status in their culture; they were outcasts, looked upon with disdain. God wanted the world to know that the Messiah had come for all people: the young and the old, the poor and the rich, the invisible and the important. The shepherds also had the task of caring for the lambs being prepared for sacrifice. Of course, how appropriate for them to be the first to know that the final, perfect sacrifice had arrived for everyone.

REFLECT AND DISCUSS:

- Think about what it would have been like to be a shepherd and to receive the angels' announcement.
- How do you think their lives were changed?

FOR YOUNGER CHILDREN:

Add the shepherds to the stable. Talk about what it must have been like to be a shepherd and to receive the angels' announcement.

NOTES:

# FOURTH THURSDAY: ANNA AND SIMEON

*Luke 2:21-39*

Two people waiting. One man and one woman, both elderly, were waiting faithfully at the temple to see the fulfillment of God's promise to Israel. They were waiting for the words of the prophet Isaiah to be a reality: "For to us a child is born, to us a son is given, and the government will be on his shoulders, and he will be called Wonderful Counselor, Mighty God, Everlasting Fathering, Prince of Peace" (Isaiah 9:6).

Imagine what would have happened if Simeon hadn't listened to the Holy Spirit's prompting to go into the temple courtyard the day that Mary and Joseph brought Jesus to be consecrated. How did Simeon know that Jesus was the One? Is it because he lived his life looking up, waiting, listening to God?

Imagine if Anna had given up worshiping and praying and fasting as she also waited. Would Mary and Joseph have received the good word and confirmation that Jesus was the "redemption of Jerusalem"? Both Simeon and Anna had been placed at the temple long before they would fulfill their work of confirming Jesus' status as the Sacrificial Lamb of Israel.

One of the ironies of this passage is that Mary and Joseph came to the temple to fulfill the Law of Moses by presenting their firstborn to the Lord as a sacrifice. The final statement begins, "When Joseph and Mary had done everything required by the Law of the Lord . . . " They could have taken the attitude that because they held the Messiah, the Son of God, in their arms, they did not need to follow the Jewish laws. But instead they fulfilled all the requirements of the law. Jesus confirmed they were right to do this when He stated: "Do not think that I have come to abolish the Law or the Prophets; I have not come to abolish them but to fulfill them" (Matthew 5:17).

REFLECT AND DISCUSS:

Whom do you most identify with—Joseph, Mary, Simeon, or Anna? Why?

FOR YOUNGER CHILDREN:

Have your children draw a picture of the scene at the temple. Talk about how each character most likely responded in the situation.

NOTES:

# FOURTH FRIDAY:
# KING HEROD AND THE MAGI

### *Matthew 2:1-23*

Two revelations. Two responses. The Magi—or wise men, as we commonly refer to them--came as a result of an eastern star to seek out the King of the Jews. They undertook a great journey at much personal cost to seek out the King. They came in faith, knowing only to follow the star. They did not know whom they were seeking. They came, and when they found the King, He was a child. But they, being overjoyed, fell down in worship and shared their valuable gifts. They responded to a warning in a dream and left the country by another way.

King Herod responded differently. He first heard about the rumored King of the Jews through the Magi. He lied and said that he too wanted to worship the King, but in reality, he felt threatened and wanted to kill Him. When he did not discover exactly the "right person who was King" he just killed anyone that could possibly have been Him.

But God always accomplishes His purposes. He may have picked Joseph to be the Messiah's earthly father because of his quick responses to the directives he received in dreams. So when Joseph dreamed Jesus was in danger, they left in the middle of the night to return to the very place where the Israelites found themselves as slaves for several centuries: Egypt. Perhaps it was a constant reminder to Mary and Joseph that Jesus came to bring God's people permanently out of slavery.

God also provided a way for Mary and Joseph to live while they were exiled to Egypt. The gifts that the Magi brought were extremely valuable. Even as they fled in the middle of the night, Mary and Joseph must have realized that God had once again provided a way where there seemed to be no way.

REFLECT AND DISCUSS:

Put yourself in Joseph and Mary's place, faced with a warning to flee your home and having to act upon it immediately.

- What would you take?
- What would bring you pain to leave behind?
- What would you feel?

FOR YOUNGER CHILDREN:

Add the wise men to the stable. Talk about who you think they were and what it would be like to take such a long journey without a map, following only a star in the sky. If it is dark, go outside, find the brightest star, and plan a pretend route for a journey.

NOTES:

# FOURTH SATURDAY: THE WITNESS AND THE WORD

*John 1:1-37*

Remember our first reading of Advent? We explored Creation and the perfect universe that God designed. He didn't create the world alone; the Word was with Him. Jesus, the Son of God, the Christmas Lamb, is the Word. In the beginning was the Word, and the Word was with God, and the Word was God. Jesus was the same at the point of Creation as He is today, and He is the same as He will be when we worship Him as the Lamb on the throne (see Revelation 5).

The whole point of Advent is found in John 1:14: "The Word became flesh and made his dwelling among us. We have seen his glory, the glory of the One and Only, who came from the Father, full of grace and truth." Jesus, who is God, was willing to set aside His status as the One and Only to come to earth. Dwell on this thought: He came to earth. God Himself came to earth. He came not as a ruler but as a servant. He came not as a king but as a baby. He came not as a priest but as the lamb to be sacrificed. Jesus is God in the flesh, who came to dwell among us, a sinful people, desperate for a lamb willing to be sacrificed so the blood can cleanse us and make us full of the Father's grace and truth.

John the Baptist knew who had come. He knew he beheld the One full of grace and truth. He knew that he, even he, as the front-runner to the Word, was unworthy to even tie His shoes. He knew that he beheld the Lamb of God in his midst. He knew that the Lamb of God came to be the Sacrificial Lamb, and as he realized the significance of the Word becoming the Sacrificial Lamb, he was struck to his knees in worship and awe. Are you as well?

**REFLECT AND DISCUSS:**

Take a moment to worship the Sacrificial Lamb, who is in your midst also. May your life be forever changed by this reality.

**FOR YOUNGER CHILDREN:**

Today is the big day! Take the baby Jesus and place Him among the animals, Mary and Joseph, the shepherds, and the wise men! Celebrate the Baby, who is God Among Us. Merry Christmas!

**NOTES:**

# EPIPHANY

# 2

PART

# CELEBRATING THE TWELVE DAYS OF EPIPHANY

DECEMBER 26: Matthew 4:1-11; 3:13-17

DECEMBER 27: John 3:1-21

DECEMBER 28: Mark 12:28-34

DECEMBER 29: Matthew 9:10-17

DECEMBER 30: John 10:1-18

DECEMBER 31: Luke 23:26-49

JANUARY 1: John 20:19-29

JANUARY 2: John 21:1-19

JANUARY 3: Acts 8:26-40; Romans 3:21-30

JANUARY 4: 1 Peter 1:18-21; 2:19-25

JANUARY 5: Hebrews 10:1-25

JANUARY 6: Revelation 5:1-14

# EPIPHANY

Feel free to continue to use the Advent wreath as you celebrate Epiphany. Or if you would prefer, use just the white Christ candle. Add other candles or decorations to enhance the visual aspect of your celebrations. You might refresh your memory about the significance of Epiphany by rereading the introduction. God bless you as you embark on discovering the joy of Epiphany!

# DECEMBER 26:
## THE TEST

*Matthew 4:1-11; 3:13-17*

John the Baptizer had predicted that one would come after him that would baptize with something far stronger than water: this One would baptize with the Holy Spirit and fire!

Shortly after that, Jesus came to John to be baptized. John did not feel worthy to baptize Jesus and tried to talk Him out of it. Jesus insisted. When He came up out of the water, a dove descended upon Him, and a voice from heaven announced, "This is my Son, whom I love; with him I am well pleased" (3:17).

Jesus had lived thirty years at that point. As far as we know, He had not done any extraordinary acts in His life. He had grown up, become a carpenter, and lived a simple life. Yet God announced from heaven that He was well pleased with His Son.

How often we feel we must do amazing acts to earn God's love. But this proclamation recorded for eternity tells us that God is well pleased with us just by our simple presence, by our very lives, by our getting up in the morning and going to bed at night. It is not what we do that matters to God--it is who we are!

Right after Jesus was baptized, He was led by the Spirit into the desert for the purpose of being tested by the Devil. Jesus fasted for forty days and forty nights, enough to make Him extremely weak, physically and probably emotionally as well. Yet His knowledge of truth gave Him enough spiritual strength to resist the Tempter and his three tests. Jesus did not fall into the pitfall of giving up His deity for bread for proof of God's existence or for a false glory that would come without going to the cross.

Often after we achieve a spiritual victory or have had a wonderful experience that leaves a lasting memory to be cherished, a test comes. Doubt creeps into our thoughts: *Perhaps God is not pleased with me* or *Maybe those leftover Christmas cookies would fill the emptiness in my soul* or *If God loved me, He would provide the money we need to pay off the Christmas presents.*

When these times come, it is important to remember the Lamb. He experienced a powerful spiritual victory and time of great blessing at His baptism, only to be led immediately into the desert to be tempted. It is easy to let our thoughts and desires go to those places of doubt and worry and unreasonable expectations. Sometimes we lead ourselves there, but often the very real voice of the Tempter does. He wants us to doubt that God is pleased with us just by our existence. He wants us to doubt that God Himself is enough for every situation.

But, like Jesus, we must remember and speak the truth, despite how weak we feel-- for God is enough, the Lamb is enough, the Truth is enough.

 REFLECT AND DISCUSS:

- Are you worn out from all the preparations of Christmas?
- Are you overwhelmed to be facing all that has been put off "until after the holidays"?
- Are you let down because Christmas is now just a memory and won't come again for another year?

Good news! The next eleven days are a continuing of the blessing of Christmas. Commit yourself to remember the truth through this time: You are special to God by your very existence, and He is enough.

 FOR YOUNGER CHILDREN:

If your children have been baptized, talk about how special it was for them to make the announcement that they wanted to follow Jesus forever. Reaffirm that commitment with them.

If your children haven't been baptized, talk to them about Jesus' baptism and how it is a model for us to follow if we want to seek after Him! Pray with them about taking the step of being baptized.

NOTES:

# DECEMBER 27:
## BORN FROM ABOVE

*John 3:1-21*

Nicodemus, it appears from this passage, was one who lived his righteousness the human way. As a Pharisee, he most likely observed every Sabbath, feast, and festival and kept every rule—and there were more than four hundred rules just to keep the Sabbath alone! He obeyed the Ten Commandments, and added some more just to be safe. He was doing his best to earn his salvation.

Jesus presents another way: salvation from above. Salvation from above means that God is the One who offers it. God is the One who accomplishes it. It does not come from anything that we can do. It comes from God. It comes from the Lamb being lifted up on the cross and sacrificed so that whoever believes in Him will inherit eternal life.

Why? Why was God willing to send His only Son into the world? To condemn the world? No. He sent His Son into the world to save the world! What, then, is our part? Jesus made it clear to Nicodemus and to us as well. "Whoever believes in [Jesus will not be] condemned, but whoever does not believe stands condemned already because he has not believed in the name of God's one and only Son" (3:18).

We don't know how Nicodemus responded that night. He may have left in a huff, wondering how anyone could be so ridiculous as to think that mere belief was enough. He may have left in confusion because the message Jesus gave was so different from what he had been taught. He may have responded to the truth and left in wonder, desiring to follow this Jesus. We do know that later he confronted some of the Pharisees on behalf of their officers who had been sent to capture Jesus but were transfixed by His words (see John 7:50-51) and that he contributed to Jesus' burial (see John 19:39).

We don't know how Nicodemus responded, but the important question is: How do you respond?

REFLECT AND DISCUSS:

- Have you, like Nicodemus, added extra requirements to your salvation?
- Do you carry around a list of rules to follow for being right with God?
- Or, do you fully believe and live out Jesus' message that your salvation comes from belief in the Lamb?

FOR YOUNGER CHILDREN:

Have your children write out the Scripture from John 3:16-17 on a poster or piece of construction paper. Put it in a place where they can see it every day. Work on memorizing the message and remembering that belief in Jesus is enough for salvation.

If your children haven't already made a decision to follow Christ, perhaps now is the time to talk to them about it. Ask if they want to make the decision to believe that Jesus is the Son of God, who came to save those who believe in Him. If they are ready, pray this simple prayer with them: Jesus, I believe that You are the Son of God and that You came to earth as the Lamb, willing to die for me. Thank You for giving me eternal life from above. Amen!

NOTES:

# DECEMBER 28:
## THE NEW RULE FOR LIFE

*Mark 12:28-34*

The commandments that Jesus stated to His listeners were not new. They came from Deuteronomy and were given shortly after the Israelites received the Ten Commandments. The statement was called the Shema, which means "to hear." It was repeated daily in Jesus' times by the Jews as they sought to follow God. This was not new news to those debating with Jesus. So, what then was the new rule for life?

The answer came from the teacher of the law who responded to Jesus' statement. He recognized that loving God and loving your neighbor "is more important than all the burnt offerings and sacrifices." This was the new news! Loving God, being in relationship with Him in our whole being--our spirit, our soul, our body, our intellect--was far more important than bringing the lamb to the altar for sacrifice.

How could this be, when the Israelites were commanded from the point of their exodus from Egypt to sacrifice animals to stay in right position with God? Of course, it was because the Sacrificial Lamb was standing in their midst. He was preparing every day of His life on earth to become the Sacrifice, which would be the permanent sacrifice, one that would last for eternity. Hebrews 9:26-28 states:

> *He has appeared once for all at the end of the ages to do away with sin by the sacrifice of himself. Just as man is destined to die once, and after that to face judgment, so Christ was sacrificed once to take away the sins of many people; and he will appear a second time, not to bear sin, but to bring salvation to those who are waiting for him.*

Jesus looked at the teacher of the law and said to him, "You are not far from the kingdom of God" (12:34). He knew that one who understood that being in relationship with God was better than offering sacrifices would be able to eventually see and believe in the Christmas Lamb as well.

REFLECT AND DISCUSS:

- Which part of your whole person has the hardest time loving God?
- Is it your mind, or is it your heart?
- Or is it in giving yourself in service?

Ask the Lord to show you where He wants to strengthen you.

 FOR YOUNGER CHILDREN:

Explain to your children that loving our neighbors is important to God. Help your children choose one neighbor for whom to do an act of kindness and what that act will be. Take a moment to pray for the neighbor you have chosen.

NOTES:

# DECEMBER 29:
## NEW CONTAINERS FOR NEW PEOPLE

*Matthew 9:10-17*

Can you imagine the religious leaders' dismay as Jesus kept hanging out with humanity's lowlife?

Tax collectors in Jerusalem were despised as traitors. Most were Jewish people who not only worked for the enemy, the Roman government, but also were crooked, taking far more tax than what was legitimate. Yet Jesus sought them out, as well as others the Pharisees considered sinners. Today the list likely would include prostitutes, alcoholics, drug addicts, beggars, people with HIV––all those society has cast off as being socially unacceptable. Yet, those were the people Jesus was seeking to hang out with. Those were the people who were throwing parties for Him and arranging for their friends to meet Him. Not so with the religious leaders; they were just plotting what their next question would be and how to trap Jesus into giving the wrong answer.

Socializing with sinners allowed Jesus to convey a major lesson on mercy and grace. Notice that the Pharisees didn't come directly to Jesus. They took a safer approach and went to His disciples, who apparently didn't have a sufficient answer. Somehow Jesus got wind of the question, and answered.

The healthy don't need a doctor; the sick do. Not only that, but God desires mercy, not sacrifice. You'll never earn your way to heaven by being more righteous than the sinner next door. You're sick; you need a doctor. There it is again. Jesus is calling people out of the old way of obeying the laws to a greater law: mercy and grace.

Even John the Baptist's disciples struggled with Jesus' answer. They couldn't figure out why Christ's disciples didn't fast as they did. Jesus used a few more analogies to help people understand the new way for a new day. Who would want to fast at a magnificent Jewish wedding while the bridegroom was still with his guests? Only after the bridegroom leaves can any fasting begin. Jesus also describes putting a new piece of cloth on an old garment—the new patch would rip from the old garment, causing worse damage. In the same way, new wine can't be poured into old wineskins. The old wineskin would burst, dumping the wine and ruining the wineskin. But if new wine is poured into new wineskins, a savory drink is available to all who desire it.

**REFLECT AND DISCUSS:**
Which part of this passage would surprise or shock you the most if you were one of the Pharisees or John's disciples listening to Jesus?

 **FOR YOUNGER CHILDREN:**
Follow through on doing the act of kindness for your neighbor. Talk to your children about how they felt when they did this act and how they think that it made their neighbor feel. If you chose a neighbor that is lonely or elderly or disabled, talk about how they showed mercy to their neighbor and how that makes Jesus happy. Pray for your neighbor again and talk about whether you would like to continue befriending him or her.

**NOTES:**

# DECEMBER 30:
## SHEPHERD OR SHEEP?

### John 10:1-18

Jesus came as the Lamb willing to be sacrificed, but He also came as the Good Shepherd who would care for the sheep. What a paradox! How could Jesus make this claim?

Perhaps it was because it was the shepherds who truly understood the sheep. Shepherds knew their sheep by name, and the sheep knew their shepherds. Often in biblical times many herds of sheep were mixed together in a sheep pen. When a shepherd came to get his flock, he would call out and only his sheep would come to the gate of the pen. The other sheep would ignore his call because he wasn't their shepherd; they did not recognize his voice. Jesus knew that those who were His sheep would recognize His call, and those who belonged to another would ignore Him.

Jesus knew also that good shepherds, those who loved their sheep, would lay down their lives for the sheep. Wild animals, storms, bandits, and thieves were all real dangers shepherds had to be willing to face, even to the point of death.

Jesus knew that danger existed for Him. He knew He was a shepherd who loved His sheep so much He would die for them. But He also knew His life wouldn't be taken from Him—He would give it willingly, as implied in verses 17-18. His words surely would have called to the "true sheep" among His listeners, who would have been familiar with Ezekiel 34:11-16:

> *For this is what the Sovereign Lord says: I myself will search for my sheep and look after them. As a shepherd looks after his scattered flock when he is with them, so will I look after my sheep. I will rescue them from all the places where they were scattered on a day of clouds and darkness. I will bring them out from the nations and gather them from the countries, and I will bring them into their own land. I will pasture them on the mountains of Israel, in the ravines and in all the settlements in the land. I will tend them in a good pasture, and the mountain heights of Israel will be their grazing land. There they will lie down in good grazing land, and there they will feed in a*

*rich pasture on the mountains of Israel. I myself will tend my sheep and have them lie down, declares the Sovereign Lord. I will search for the lost and bring back the strays. I will bind up the injured and strengthen the weak, but the sleek and the strong I will destroy. I will shepherd the flock with justice.*

That is how the Lamb can also be the shepherd. Jesus came as one who would love His flock so much He was willing to die for it. He was willing to be the Lamb in place of all the others so they would be given life instead of death.

**REFLECT AND DISCUSS:**

What does it mean to you that the One who is the Good Shepherd is also willing to be the Sacrificial Lamb? Think about where you are willing to become sacrificial for the sake of God's kingdom.

 **FOR YOUNGER CHILDREN:**

Look for some appropriate resources with which to study sheep, and use this time to understand more about sheep's characteristics and how they respond to the one who cares for them.

**NOTES:**

# DECEMBER 31:
## THE SACRIFICE

*Luke 23:26-49*

The Lamb hung on the cross. Unlike the temple sacrifices in which the animal died quickly and without suffering, this Lamb hung and bled and suffered. Unlike the temple sacrifices in which the animals didn't understand their fate, this Lamb suffered the humiliation of being mocked and jeered and rejected. Unlike the temple sacrifices in which the animals died anonymously, this Lamb had a sign over Him that read, "This is the King of the Jews."

But what king hangs on a cross, rejected by his people? Only the Lamb. Only the King who chose the good of His people over His own life. This King, having had mercy even in His greatest suffering, offered forgiveness and hope to one criminal while the other criminal joined in the crowd's jeering and insults.

This was a dark time for Jerusalem. This was a dark time for the world. It was such a dark time that it literally became dark in the middle of the day for three hours. The king of darkness must have been throwing a party, believing that he had won the battle. He must have believed that the God of the Heavens had been defeated and that it was he himself who had won--that the Lamb had been sacrificed, never to be heard of again.

But in the midst of the darkness, the temple curtain supernaturally tore from top to bottom. Once one piece of fabric, it became two. Jerusalem became light again. The world became light again. The Lamb called out in a loud voice, "Father, into your hands I commit my spirit" (23:46). Then His body went still.

Unlike the temple sacrifices in which the animals had no choice in their fate to become sacrifices, this Lamb had a choice. He was not crucified. He gave Himself to be crucified. He gave Himself willingly to be the Sacrificial Lamb, whose blood will forever cleanse God's people and set them free. Praise be to God.

**REFLECT AND DISCUSS:**

What is the significance of the temple curtain being torn from top to bottom? (The curtain separated the Holy Place and the Most Holy Place in the temple. The curtain was a visible barrier for everyday people to have access to Almighty God because only once a year, on the Day of Atonement, could the high priest go past the curtain.)

 **FOR YOUNGER CHILDREN:**

Ask your children to remember a time when they got hurt. Think about how much it hurt. Talk about all the ways that Jesus hurt when He hung on the cross, and tell your children that it is because He loved them so much He was willing to go through all His suffering. Pray with your children, thanking Jesus for His pain for them.

**NOTES:**

# JANUARY 1:
## "PEACE BE WITH YOU"

### John 20:19-29

Can you imagine the scene? All the disciples huddled together in a secret upper room, fearing any moment they would hear a loud pounding on the door—the religious leaders coming to harass them and possibly arrest them. Instead, Jesus went and stood among them. He didn't have to pound on the door for it to be opened; His resurrected body just went through it!

Jesus didn't harass the disciples, nor did He rebuke them for betraying Him in His greatest hour of need. Instead, He spoke these words: "Peace be with you." It is hard to appreciate how those words must have sounded to the disciples when they were fearing for their very lives or even feeling so dejected because they had fled from their Lord when He was arrested. *Peace be with you. Peace be with you. Peace be with you.* The room must have been flooded with rest, hope, and joy when Jesus arrived, but, most of all, it was flooded with peace.

Thomas wasn't present that first time Jesus appeared to the disciples. Why was that? Was it because he was braver than the rest and He didn't need to hide in an upper room? Was it because he was taking care of the practical needs by buying food for their dinner? Or was it that God had a higher purpose in his absence?

When Thomas returned, the disciples had a chance to testify to Jesus' appearance. Thomas got to hear the words Jesus said, how He looked, and how He came into the room. However, as Thomas was practical by nature, he chose to respond in the flesh. He chose to respond by doubt. He chose to respond by saying he needed physical proof.

Have you ever been in a similar situation? A fellow believer told you a story that required faith to believe. You saw the change in the person, but you just couldn't quite believe the way the change appeared—that is, through supernatural events. So, either outwardly or inwardly you began to question the person's faith and sanity. You thought to yourself, *If I could have just seen it, then I could believe—but I didn't see it, so I will have to keep wondering if it is really true.*

A week later Jesus reappeared to His disciples in the very same room. Thomas did see and he believed. He had physical proof and fell to his knees calling out, "My Lord and my God!" Jesus, however, told Thomas, "Now you've seen me so you believe. But how blessed are those who have not seen and yet believe."

Perhaps the higher purpose for Thomas' original absence was so we can all recognize ourselves in Thomas. We want to understand God's ways. We want to see Him working. We want to audibly hear Jesus say the words "Peace be with you," instead of just believing He is speaking them to us. He wants us to believe without physical proof that we are His beloved, that no condemnation exists for those who believe, and that He is continually blessing us with His peace.

## REFLECT AND DISCUSS:

Jesus spoke "Peace be with you" three times to His disciples when they were so afraid.

- What are you afraid of?
- What upper room are you hiding in?

Ask Jesus to show you His peace and give you faith to believe He is standing right next to you saying the words, Peace be with you. Peace be with you. Peace be with you.

##  FOR YOUNGER CHILDREN:

Get a note card and write out the Scripture from Philippians 4:6-7 on it. Help your children begin to memorize it and let go of anxiety by presenting all things to God with thanks. God promises to guard our hearts and minds in Christ Jesus. Talk to your children about how Jesus can be anywhere, and explain that He is right next to them at all times, so they do not have to be afraid.

## NOTES:

# JANUARY 2:
## "FEED MY SHEEP"

*John 21:1-19*

Imagine how the disciples felt catching nothing after an entire night of fishing. They'd been hiding in the room for a long time, and finally had gathered the courage to venture out to do what they did best: fish. And yet, they had fished all night and came up dry. Do you think they felt discouraged, abandoned, hopeless, tired, and downhearted?

Just as they were coming in, a man stood on the shore and called out to them, "Friends, did you catch any fish?" He offered some advice after He heard their negative answer. "Throw your nets on the right side of the boat." Here these men were expert fishermen; they had just exhausted themselves and all their skills without success; it was daylight, which meant fish headed for the bottom of the lake—and this anonymous beachcomber was giving them advice. Amazingly, the disciples took it, and the catch was the biggest of their fishing careers. It was so big they could barely get it in the boat, and yet the net never tore. Suddenly, they knew that this stranger was Jesus.

Now, put yourself in Peter's place. Remember that he had denied even knowing Jesus to a whole gathering of people and Jesus heard the denial. He had abandoned Jesus almost immediately after swearing to be willing to die with Him. On that morning would you have turned away and hoped that Jesus would just kind of miss you? Often when we have failed we want to want to hide, to become invisible, to disappear. Not Peter. He jumped out of the boat and ran through the water, straight to Jesus! This was the wonderful aspect of Peter's character; he boldly lived life, even when he had just failed.

Once again, the Lamb became the Shepherd who cares for His flock. Jesus asked Peter "Simon, son of John, do you love me?" Peter was still Simon; he was not yet the Rock that Jesus had named him earlier. He had to first be restored. It was through the restoration process and the communion with Jesus that Simon son of John became the Rock! Jesus gave Peter three opportunities to affirm his love for Jesus, and Jesus gave Peter three opportunities to accept his future mission "to care for the flock!" Peter was told to feed the Shepherd's lambs, take care of the Shepherd's sheep, and feed the Shepherd's sheep. This is amazing. The one who had just days earlier totally failed the Lord was being given responsibility for the Shepherd's flock, His most valuable possession. Peter accepted the mission because he knew he was secure in his Savior's love.

 REFLECT AND DISCUSS:

Remember a time when you felt that you really failed, and think about what you did after the event.

- Did you run and hide from people?
- Did you run and hide from God?
- Or did you turn and run to Jesus, the One who always has His arms out open and wide for you to be loved well and then restored to your proper place as His beloved disciple?

 FOR YOUNGER CHILDREN:

Talk to your children about times when they have failed.

- How did they feel?
- How did they think you viewed their failure?

Talk to your children about how Jesus responded to Peter. Explain to them that Jesus offers peace, not condemnation. Spend time together thanking Jesus for His ability to forgive and restore.

NOTES:

# JANUARY 3: GOD'S EXPANDED BOUNDARIES NOW A REALITY

### Acts 8:26-40; Romans 3:21-30

Earlier in Advent we explored the requirement in the law that kept eunuchs from worshiping at the temple. A prophecy in Isaiah 56 states that eunuchs would be given a memorial and a name better than sons and daughters. Those who read this prophecy in the days before Jesus must have shaken their heads in disbelief, for to have eunuchs and foreigners worshiping at the temple was unheard of; it was "unclean."

But in Acts we find that God kept His promise. We read of a man named Philip who was told to walk south to the road that lead to Gaza. Philip didn't question the angel. He just started walking! He discovered the purpose for his walk when he found an important Ethiopian official, but a eunuch nonetheless, reading the book of Isaiah. Philip did what any astute evangelist did: He asked a question to start a conversation. A marvelous exchange followed.

All his life the Ethiopian had been unable to engage anyone to answer his questions about spiritual matters. God sent one of His best men to explain the story of the Sacrificial Lamb. When the eunuch heard it, he knew he wanted what the Lamb could offer, so he asked Philip, "What is to stop me from being baptized?" Actually, the man most likely expected the answer every righteous Jew would give: what stopped him from being baptized was his being a eunuch.

Yet Philip understood that the boundaries expanded when the Lamb was sacrificed. He understood that Jesus came to save the sick, the outcasts, the unforgivables, the hungry, and the seeking. And the eunuch was hungry and he was seeking. This is the attitude of heart God wants--those who know their need for Him and for the Lamb.

REFLECT AND DISCUSS:

Think about what it must have been like to be a eunuch in the time this was written.

- What must it have felt like for the Ethiopian eunuch to have heard of the Lamb's love and invitation for relationship?
- Who in your life needs to hear the same story?

Commit yourself to look for God-given opportunities to share as Philip did with the eunuch.

 FOR YOUNGER CHILDREN:

Play a game where everyone waits with their eyes closed while one person goes and hides. When everyone opens their eyes, they'll notice that the person is gone. Then, everyone closes their eyes again, and the "missing" person comes back in the room. When everyone opens their eyes again, it feels as though the person appeared out of nowhere. Do it over and over, all the while talking to your children about how God can do anything, even things such as taking Philip away from the Ethiopian and having Philip reappear in another city.

NOTES:

# JANUARY 4: REDEEMED BY THE BLOOD OF THE LAMB

### *1 Peter 1:18-21; 2:19-25*

Think about a time when you have been unjustly accused. How did you feel? How did you respond? How did you want to respond? As Americans our Constitution tells us we are entitled to "life, liberty, and the pursuit of happiness." How does this compare with Jesus, the Lamb that came to earth with the sole purpose of suffering?

Remember Peter? He took the easy road when he lied about knowing and following Jesus. After Jesus restored him, Peter understood that suffering for the Lamb was the "greatest privilege" he could ever possess. He wrote about the Lamb's suffering and our suffering in his first book written to God's people scattered throughout the world (see 1 Peter 1:1).

Jesus redeemed His people, not by anything money could ever buy, but through His blood. Jesus, the Lamb without blemish or defect, was the Sacrifice that satisfied God's justice. Jesus, the Lamb, never committed a sin, yet He suffered on the tree on which He hung. However, He never spoke back, He never retaliated, He made no threats. Instead, He trusted the character of His Father, He trusted the process that was designed before the creation of the world, He trusted that His blood would be enough to heal God's chosen people.

How does the awareness of this truth change our lives? Does it cause us to be willing to let go of our rights and instead suffer as Jesus did? Does it heal us enough that we don't respond out of our own issues, but instead can respond through Christ's love? Does it give us faith enough to believe that God will deal justly with those who have wounded us and caused us to suffer? Does the blood of the Lamb bring us to freedom?

What did Peter say is the outcome for us, and for the saints who have walked before us, that the blood of the Lamb was shed? In 1 Peter 2:9-10, we are told:

> *But you are a chosen people, a royal priesthood, a holy nation, a people belonging to God, that you may declare the praises of him who called you out of darkness into his wonderful light. Once you were not a people, but now you are the people of God; once you had not received mercy, but now you have received mercy.*

This is the good news of our faith! We are chosen, we are royal, we are holy, we are a people that belongs to God! We have received His mercy, so that we may walk in His light—and show the rest of the world the way to know the Lamb as well.

 REFLECT AND DISCUSS:

Think about which one of the titles means the most to you: being chosen, being royal, being holy, or being a people who belongs to God. Why?

- Take some time to consider how our status can allow us to live with a greater amount of mercy toward others.
- Whom do you need to extend this mercy to today?

 FOR YOUNGER CHILDREN:

Think with your children about what it means to be part of a family.

- What privileges come with it?
- What responsibilities?
- What significance does a last name carry?

Now think about what it means to be part of God's family: to be the people of God.

- What privileges does this bring?
- What responsibilities?

If your children are old enough, have them write letters to God thanking Him for the privilege of being part of His family. If they are too young, have them draw a picture of what the family of God looks like to them.

NOTES:

# JANUARY 5:
## AT THE RIGHT HAND OF GOD

*Hebrews 10:1-25*

Jesus understood His mission when He came to earth. He knew that physical healings were important; He knew that speaking truth was important; He knew that raising up leaders to carry on the mission after He left was important; but He also knew the true reason that He came to earth. It was to become the final sacrifice for sins. It was to be the Sacrificial Lamb. In Hebrews 10:8-10 He states:

> *"Sacrifices and offerings, burnt offerings and sin offerings you did not desire, nor were you pleased with them" (although the law required them to be made). Then he said, "Here I am, I have come to do your will." He sets aside the first to establish the second. And by that will, we have been made holy through the sacrifice of the body of Jesus Christ once for all.*

Jesus understood that His sacrifice was enough, that it was all that was needed for every person who believes to be made holy and acceptable in God's eyes. This was His mission; this is why He came to earth; this is why He willingly died.

When He completed the mission, He was invited to sit at the right hand of the throne of His Father. However, He did not sit there in order to judge those who believed; He sat there to give mercy and grace and to invite us to the throne as well, as written in Hebrews 4:14-16:

> *Therefore, since we have a great high priest who has gone through the heavens, Jesus the Son of God, let us hold firmly to the faith we profess. For we do not have a high priest who is unable to sympathize with our weaknesses, but we have one who has been tempted in every way, just as we are--yet was without sin. Let us then approach the throne of grace with confidence, so that we may receive mercy and find grace to help us in our time of need.*

In those moments when we feel fragile, uncertain, unacceptable, or unlovable, we must remember the truth. Jesus is the Great High Priest who has come to earth and knows from experience that we are weak, that we are tempted to sin, and that we are in desperate need of His mercy and grace. He invites us to the throne of grace so we may come confidently to Him to receive His mercy, His grace, and His strength in our times of need. He has finished His work and now He waits for us to come—to the throne!

### REFLECT AND DISCUSS:

Think about what it means to be invited to the throne of grace where the Lamb is seated at the right hand of God the Almighty.

- How is this different from the way those in Old Testament times lived?
- How does this truth change your view of God?
- How does this truth strengthen your faith?

Make a decision now to go straight to the throne of grace the next time you feel needy or weak or sinful, so that you might receive mercy and find grace to help you in your time of need.

### FOR YOUNGER CHILDREN:

Tell the story of Cinderella or remind your children of it. Talk about how we are like Cinderella, living in poor circumstances until the prince invites us to the ball. We go, and we are awed by how wonderful the palace is and how kind and loving the prince is toward us. When we run away from the prince, he leaves the palace and comes to get us so that we might always be together with him. Celebrate that Cinderella is now the princess, and we are as well, as we are always invited to the throne in the palace.

 NOTES:

# JANUARY 6:
## WORTHY IS THE LAMB

### Revelation 5:1-14

From the beginning of time, anticipation of this moment has existed. From the first time God the Father slew the animals to clothe Adam and Eve, to the time the sacrificial system was developed for the Israelites, to the time when Jesus Himself came to earth, was crucified, died, and then was resurrected, anticipation of this moment has existed.

The Lamb was on the throne. The four living creatures and twenty-four elders sang a new song to the Lamb:

> *You are worthy to take the scroll*
> *and to open its seals,*
> *because you were slain,*
> *and with your blood you purchased people for God*
> *from every tribe and language and people and nation.*
> *You have made them to be a kingdom of priests to serve our God,*
> *and they will reign on the earth. (Revelation 5:9-10)*

This was only the beginning of the greatest and most glorious worship to the Lamb. The angels came, numbering thousands upon thousands, and then ten thousand times ten thousand. They encircled the throne and the living creatures and the elders. They sang out in a loud voice, "Worthy is the Lamb, who was slain, to receive power and wealth and wisdom and strength and honor and glory and praise!" (5:12).

This wasn't all, however. Every creature in heaven and on earth and under the earth and on the sea, all of creation, was singing: "To him who sits on the throne and to the Lamb be praise and honor and glory and power, forever and ever!" (5:13). The four living creatures said, "Amen," and the elders fell down and worshiped.

We are there. All who believe are at the throne of the Lamb who was slain. All those who refuse to believe will also be present—saddened that they rejected the Lamb while they lived. They will leave, but all who believe will stay and worship. For we are a kingdom, we are priests who serve the Living God, and we will reign on the earth. We are the Saints, made whole and holy by the blood of the Lamb that was slain. We are forever grateful. Amen.

## REFLECT AND DISCUSS:

- What does it means to be a saint?

Spend time praising the Lamb that was slain. Anticipate the moment when all of creation will bow to the Lamb, and begin to practice this glorious worship today.

## FOR YOUNGER CHILDREN:

Have your children draw a picture of or write about how they envision Revelation 5 will happen. If you own a CD of the "Hallelujah" chorus from Handel's Messiah or "Agnus Dei" by Amy Grant or Michael W. Smith, play it while they write or draw. If you are listening to the "Hallelujah" chorus, stand up when the choir sings the hallelujah section! Take a moment to thank the Lamb for being willing to come as the Christmas Lamb.

## NOTES:

# A FINAL WORD

Before I finished writing the final day of this book, I felt the Lord impressing me to come and spend time in worship. Being a rather goal-oriented person, I had to consider the invitation for a moment before I realized what an opportunity I had just been given. The Sacrificial Lamb was inviting me to commune with Him and consider again how great His sacrifice for me.

I spent about thirty minutes in one of the most powerful times of worship I have ever experienced. I caught a glimpse of the reality of the Lamb standing at the throne in the final days. I heard a small sound of the magnificent singing around the throne. I realized again what a privilege I've been given because the Lamb was willing to be slain for me! His blood is what allows me to be God's child, and it is enough.

His blood is enough for you too! It is the reason Jesus was willing to come to earth as a baby—so that you might live forever with Him.

My hope for this book is to help each of us walk in a greater reality of the incredible invitation we have—to join the long list of believers that have come before us, and will come after us, at the throne of the Lamb for eternity.

# NOTES

1. Walter Brueggemann, Interpretation: A Bible Commentary for Teaching and Preaching (Atlanta: John Knox Press, 1982), pp. 81-83.

2. Brueggemann, pp. 85-86.

3. Eugene H. Peterson, from the introduction to Leviticus, The Message: The Old Testament Books of Moses (Colorado Springs, Colo.: NavPress Publishing Group, 2001), p. 166.

# URL LINKS

http://www.reclaimidentity.org

http://www.ebookannie.com

"Hallelujah"  https://www.youtube.com/watch?v=IUZEtVbJT5c

"Agnus Dei"  https://www.youtube.com/watch?v=HPBmFwBSGb0

# ABOUT THE AUTHOR

Tamara J. Buchan, founder and director of Reclaim Ministries, ordained Evangelical Covenant pastor, author and speaker, holds a Master of Divinity from Denver Seminary. However, these worldly credentials do not fulfill or thrill her nearly as much as her Identity as a Beloved Child and Royal Heir in God's Family. Tamara is passionate about relationships, especially her husband and family. Tamara and Bill live in beautiful Sonoma County, California. To find out more about how you can Reclaim your Identity, Life and Destiny, visit **www.facebook.com/ReclaimIdentity**. To register for the transformational Reclaim Identity Retreat in Sonoma County, visit **www.ReclaimIdentity.org**.

# THANK YOU

Thank you for reading *Seeking the Christmas Lamb*. The Advent and Epiphany season is a wonderful time to anticipate Christ's coming and the freedom He brings with His arrival. If you enjoyed this book, you may enjoy *Identity Crisis: Reclaim the True You* and our new 12-Book Series, *You were Meant for More: Green Embraces: Identity Reclaimed and Spun Out on Shame?* Reclaim Your Sanity are the first books of the 12- Book Series, *You were Meant for More*. This 12 Book Series is written for the Millennial generation, but has a powerful impact on people of all generations.

Join us for our monthly Reclaim Ministry Interactive Conference calls, a platform hosting special guests, updates, support and encouragement. Bring your questions, testimonies and prayers as we share key insights, personal testimonies, and pray together. There will a Q & A Session at the end of each session allowing you time to ask your questions. Join us! If interested, contact us at **www.reclaimidentity.org/contact.html** and we will email you the conference call phone number/code, time zone to connect together. Invite a friend! Explore our social media links and receive additional devotional tips, resources, and recipes for Reclaiming your Identity, Life and Destiny.

# IDENTITY CRISIS: RECLAIM THE TRUE YOU

What does a dried dandelion have to do with an identity crisis? Everything, if we stop looking at it from a gardener's perspective and start to understand its hidden value. The identities we adopt from the world are like dandelions the gardener fervently attacks before they dry up into the perfect ball of seeds, which spread all over the yard when the wind begins to blow. If we think about our enemy, the Devil, as the gardener, we begin to understand his motive is to convince us that our identities are worthless weeds: throwaways when compared to the beautiful rose bushes right next to us. Our enemy, the gardener, thrives when we agree that our identities are discarded weeds, rather than boldly reclaiming our true identities from our Master Gardener: the Creator of the Universe. To reclaim is to take that which is worthless and make it beautiful and productive again. An overgrown garden with dried dandelions can appear to be worthless. However, when the Master Gardener begins to blow the seeds, our lives suddenly "wake up" and start to take root in gardens we never dreamed we could inhabit.

*Available in Paperback and eBook*

# IDENTITY CRISIS: RECLAIM THE TRUE YOU
# COMPANION BIBLE STUDY: PART ONE

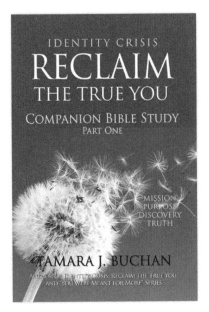

*Identity Crisis: Reclaim the True You Study Guide* is a 6-week daily process designed to support you as you journey towards reclaiming your Identity, Life and Destiny because you truly were "Meant for More!"

It takes 90 days to build a new brain path, so *Identity Crisis: Reclaim the True You Study Guide* builds on the process of creating new dreams that replace the worn out defeated thoughts that often keep us paralyzed. Partner together with God to discover just how much He is intent on Reclaiming your Identity, Life and Destiny because He knows "You are Meant for More!"

*Available in Paperback and eBook*

# "You were Meant for More" series
## *GREEN EMBRACES: IDENTITY RECLAIMED*

A strong handshake, a tender hug, a long embrace...being held feels good. As human beings built for connection, embraces carry power when they come from someone who knows us fully and loves us anyways. The embrace of God's powerfully loving arms began in a green garden long ago. The original design was a clean, lively, and green creation to host and hold people as they were meant to be. To live loved was the original design. We've wandered and gotten lost, lived for less, and walked a winding road. However, the fresh, pure, living embrace of God who knows us as Beloved Child, is available to each of us, right now. It's up to us to reclaim what was ours all along.

Discover that we are truly loved, that our story is part of a greater divine story, that we are forgiven and truly accepted and that we have a true place of belonging. If embraced, these words have the power to bring true freedom, the kind of freedom that can only come when we see ourselves the way that God sees us, a beloved child of the King!

*Available in paperback book and eBook*

# "You were Meant for More" series
## *SPUN OUT ON SHAME? RECLAIM YOUR SANITY*

Shame literally spins us around as isolation, hopelessness, and self-condemnation, become our constant companions. God breaks into the cycle, taking our shame and spinning it into his forgiveness. As we are cleansed and set free, our lives become fresh and fully alive. Spun out on shame? Reclaim Your Sanity, will take you through a journey of exchanging shame for freedom...the life you were meant to experience...You were Meant for More!

Just as washed clothes are hung out to dry in the fresh air, likewise, God wants us to experience a fresh start by going through His "wash cycle," spun out to dry, and then hung in the fresh air. As He washes us with water of His Word, dirty shame is removed for a clean, fresh start...living an abundant life He always meant for us to live!

*Available in paperback book and eBook*

# "YOU WERE MEANT FOR MORE" SERIES
## *OUR DAD IS NOT MAD: TRUST RECLAIMED*

We look out into all the world and see suffering all around us. We wonder what kind of a dad would allow his child to experience a world like this, one full of pain and torment. It's pretty simple to assume that our Dad is Mad.

Perhaps the suffering isn't only out there, but on the inside. Perhaps it was your earthly dad as he betrayed your trust, crushed your spirit, or abused your body. In your child-like state, you couldn't help but make the connection that your heavenly dad is just like your earthly dad, he's mad.

Maybe you were lucky and had an amazing dad. But, life happened, and as one challenging experience after another hit you, the thought began to emerge more often that you must have done something wrong and your dad must be...mad.

Believing our heavenly dad is not mad, but is good and trustworthy is one of the greatest challenges of life. Journey through Our Dad is Not Mad: Trust Reclaimed and discover a trustworthy father who loves you beyond what you could ever imagine.

*Available in paperback book and eBook*

# "YOU WERE MEANT FOR MORE" SERIES
## 5-STAGES OF IDENTITY: SUCCESS RECLAIMED

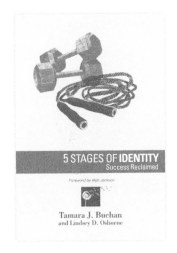

Success. The world tells us to believe that success is defined by what we do or by the things we own, but Jesus came to show us a different way to live success. He flipped the order. He taught us to know first WHO we are, and to let our True Identity define our success. Think about it. When Jesus died, he didn't have a job, he didn't own a home, or even a car. He alienated most of the important people around him, two of his friends betrayed him—and most of his other disciples quickly disappeared when he was arrested. Despite it all, if you look for a "Top 10 Most Successful People" in history, you will ALWAYS find Jesus on the list. Why? Jesus understood that success came through living in relationship, first with his loving father, and then with the people around him. He knew the way to the top was to serve and even to sacrifice his life for his friends.

5 Stages of Identity: Success Reclaimed redefines success through the exploration of Jesus' every day life. Jesus modeled valuable lessons for us in each stage of identity. His actions help us identify the pitfalls, give us strategies for the challenges, and provide us with tips for how to navigate the route through earthly success and failure. When we apply Jesus' practical lessons to our lives, we discover ourselves reaching for a success, which ultimately satisfies the longings of our hearts.

Are you ready? Put on your workout clothes so you can exercise reclaimed success at every stage in your identity journey, enabling you to leave your significant imprint upon the world!

*Coming soon to Paperback and eBook*

CPSIA information can be obtained
at www.ICGtesting.com
Printed in the USA
FSOW03n1553281015
12707FS